The Quilts of Gee's Bend

SUSAN GOLDMAN RUBIN

Abrams Books for Young Readers
New York

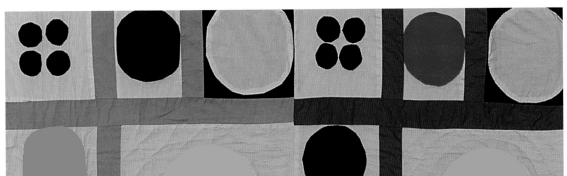

To my friend Ann Whitford Paul, writer and quilter

Cataloging-in-Publication Data has been applied for and may be obtained from the Library of Congress.

ISBN: 978-1-4197-2131-1

Text copyright © 2017 Susan Goldman Rubin
For illustration credits, see page 53.
Book design by Melissa J. Barrett

Printed and bound in China
10 9 8 7 6 5 4 3 2 1

Abrams Books for Young Readers are available at special discounts when purchased in
quantity for premiums and promotions as well as fundraising or educational use. Special editions can
also be created to specification. For details, contact specialsales@abramsbooks.com or the address below.

ABRAMS The Art of Books
115 West 18th Street, New York, NY 10011
abramsbooks.com

The Area of Gee's Bend, Alabama

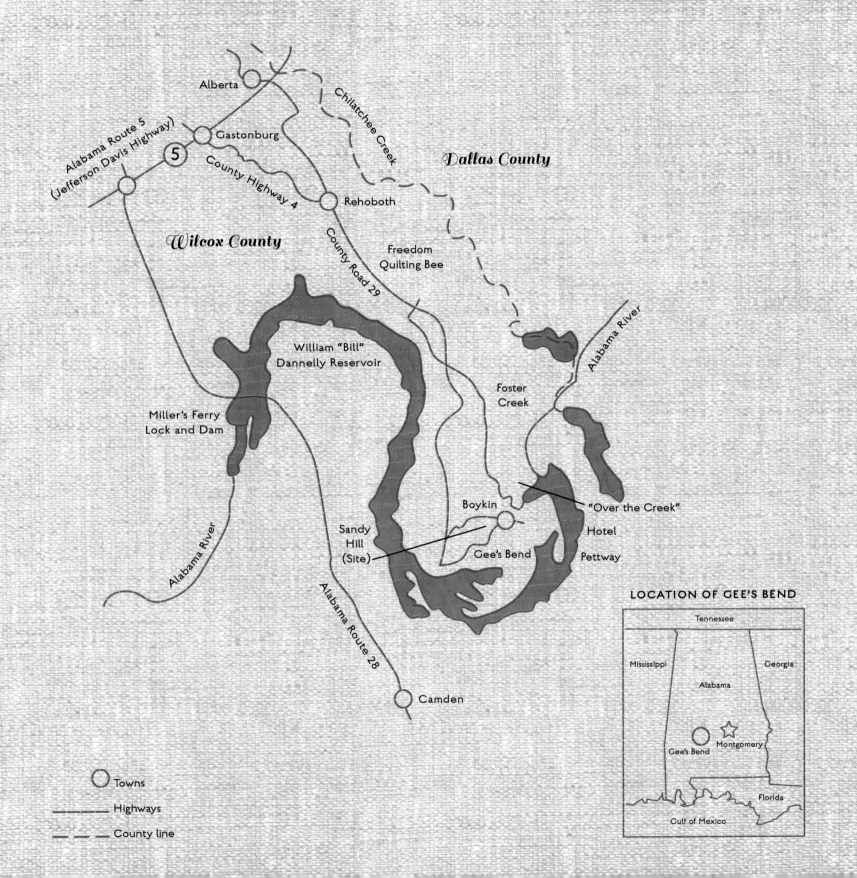

Alberta

Chilatchee Creek

Dallas County

Alabama Route 5 (Jefferson Davis Highway)

5

Gastonburg

County Highway 4

Rehoboth

Wilcox County

Freedom Quilting Bee

County Road 29

Alabama River

William "Bill" Dannelly Reservoir

Miller's Ferry Lock and Dam

Foster Creek

Alabama River

"Over the Creek"

Boykin

Hotel

Sandy Hill (Site)

Gee's Bend

Pettway

Alabama River

Alabama Route 28

Camden

LOCATION OF GEE'S BEND

Tennessee

Mississippi

Georgia

Alabama

Gee's Bend

Montgomery

Florida

Gulf of Mexico

○ Towns

— Highways

- - - County line

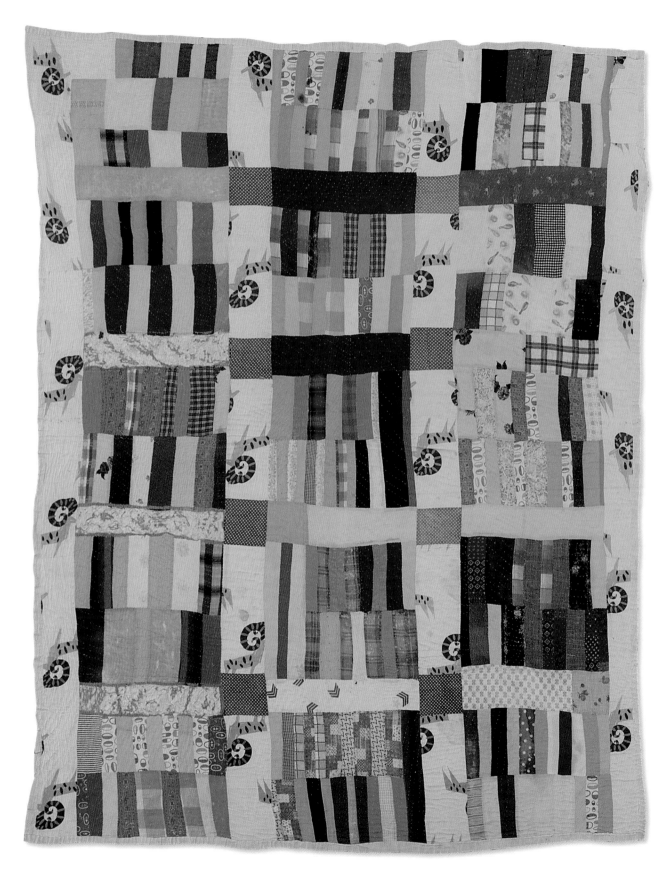

"Stacked Bricks," 1928, Nettie Young.

"One Patch," "Diamonds" variation, circa 1975, Mary L. Bennett.

When Nettie Young

was eleven years old, her mother gave her a pile of cloth strips and told her to make a quilt all by herself. Nettie had always sat with her mother and watched her quilting, picking up the scraps at her feet, but this time her mother walked away. She was testing her daughter to see if she was independent as well as talented. The cotton and corduroy scraps were in different colors and patterns: plaids, checks, dots, even a little yellow animal print. The odds and ends came

from old work shirts, dress tails, and aprons. Looking back, at age eighty-nine, Nettie said, "When I was growing up, you threw nothing away. . . . You found every good spot for a quilt piece, and that's how you made your quilts."

Nettie arranged the strips to form squares in a brilliant geometric design. She called her finished quilt "Stacked Bricks." From then on, she became known as one of the best quilters in Gee's Bend, Alabama.

ABOVE Mary L. Bennett, 2000.

BELOW Descendants of former slaves of the Pettway Plantation, 1937.

"I always loved sewing," she said. "Didn't need a pattern . . . I just draw it out the way I want it."

Mary L. Bennett also began on her own. "Didn't nobody teach me to make quilts," she said. "I just learned it by myself, about twelve or thirteen. I was seeing my grandmamma piecing it up, and then I start. I just taken me some pieces and put it together, piece them up till they look like I want them to look."

The women of Gee's Bend have been making quilts for generations. They are descended from the slaves on the Pettway Plantation. In 1845, Mark Pettway moved his family and more than one hundred slaves from North Carolina to Gee's Bend, along the Alabama River. The bulb of land is five miles wide and seven miles long and is surrounded by water on three sides. The place got its name from Joseph Gee, a white planter who had staked his claim there in 1816.

After the end of the Civil War, many of the freed slaves took the last name Pettway and stayed in Gee's Bend, forming their own all-black community. The old slave quarter grew into a village. In 1900, a white lawyer named Adrian Van de Graaff bought the plantation, and the Gee's Benders worked the land for him as tenant farmers. "The same Negroes and their descendants are upon it who tilled it as slaves," Van de Graaff wrote to a friend. The Gee's Benders continued to "work like slaves for the white people," said Loretta Pettway.

Aunt Nellie Pettway carrying wood for the fireplace from the yard, 1939.

Six days a week, the women went out to the fields along with the men. They hoed, plowed, and picked cotton and yams. But as they bent over cotton stalks, they thought about their quilts. At the end of the day, while they did chores at home and cooked dinner, they composed patterns in their heads. Pieces of cloth that had been tucked away safely were brought out at night, when, at last, it was time for quilting. "We had no radio, no TV, no nothing," recalled Mary Lee Bendolph. "That's the way we learned—sitting watching our mamas piecing the quilt. When the sun came down, you be in the house together, laughing and talking. We were more blessed then."

Many of the African American women in Gee's Bend learned how to make quilts from their mothers, grandmothers, and aunts. Mary Lee's daughter, Essie Bendolph Pettway, is in the fourth generation of quilt makers in her family. Essie said, "I was looking at my mama sewing back when I was seven, eight—might have been younger—and I was thinking, I want to do that for myself." Essie made her first quilt in 1968, when she was twelve. Right away, she showed extraordinary talent. When she was seventeen, she made a quilt called "One Patch," which features bars of blue (from denim work shirts) and white (from flour sacks) on one side, and has stacked squares and rectangles in all sorts of colors and patterns, including a sliver of printed flowers, on the other. As an adult, Essie used remnants from dresses she had sewn for herself and her mother in a green leaf print to make her vibrant quilt "Pinwheel," whose triangles in shades of green and blue seem to be spinning against the leaves.

Essie Bendolph Pettway, 1939.

"When we got nine or ten years old, [our mother] gave us a needle and a thimble and told us to quilt, and that's why we quilted so much," said Arlonzia Pettway. Her mother, Missouri Pettway, showed

"Housetop" variation, circa 1965, Mary L. Bennett.

Front of "One Patch," a two-sided quilt, blocks, stacked squares, and rectangles variation, 1973, Essie Bendolph Pettway.

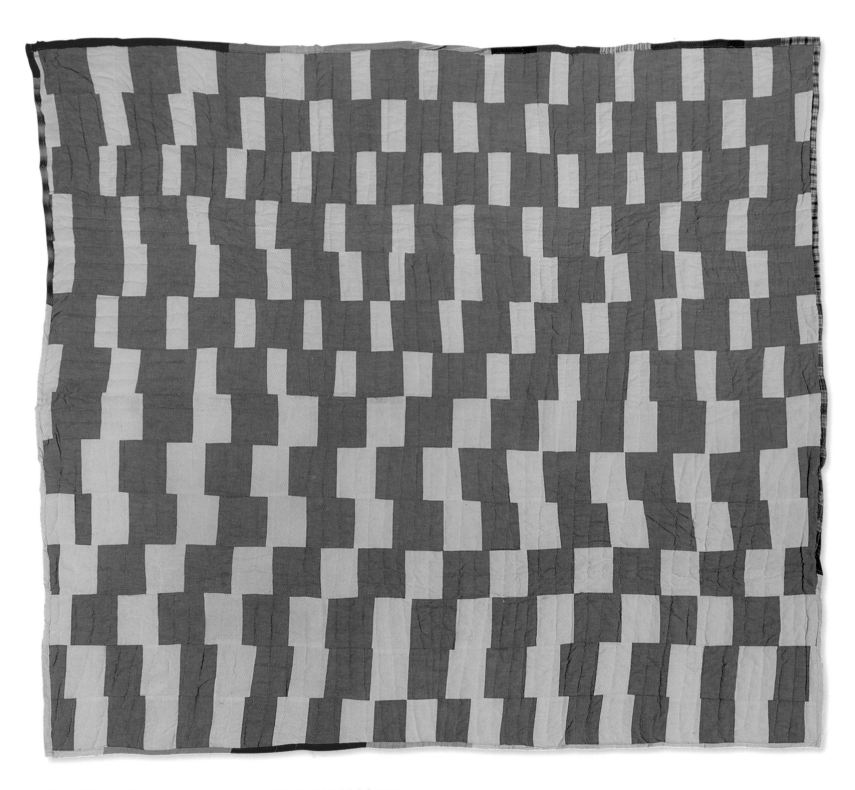

Back of "One Patch"; cotton, polyester knit, denim; 1973, Essie Bendolph Pettway.

ABOVE Mary Lee Bendolph, 2002.
RIGHT "Pinwheel" variation, 2000, Essie Bendolph Pettway.

her the basics. One of Arlonzia's masterpieces is a "Housetop" quilt that has nine blocks bursting with color. Each block contains wide and narrow strips of bright red that frame a wild assortment of patterns. Yet the design holds the ravishing array together.

Some of the bold geometric patterns have been handed down. Loretta Pettway said, "I just made what my grandmamma had made back in those days—'Bricklayer,' 'Housetop,' and stuff." But the quilters created their own fresh versions of traditional designs like "Log Cabin" and "Star."

Mary L. Bennett's "Housetop" quilts, for instance, are all different. One of them features four squares made of strips in bold colors: red, golden yellow, pink

"Housetop," nine-block variation, 1982, Arlonzia Pettway.

plaid, and black. Another has nine blocks of dark blue and white framed by checked materials.

How did the women come up with original ideas? Annie Mae Young said, "You find the colors and the shapes and certain fabrics that work out right, kind of like working a puzzle." Mary Lee Bendolph remembered that her mother would sit under a tree and wait for inspiration. The pattern of a quilt would come to her in a dream.

The women made quilts to keep their families warm. Their log cabins were miserably cold and drafty. Dust and damp air from the Alabama River rose between the gaping floorboards. "You could see the ground through the floor," recalled Annie Bell Pettway. "You could look outside through the wall."

The children slept on top of quilts, under quilts, and wrapped up in quilts. As many as six or seven quilts layered the corn husk–filled mattresses. More quilts covered the walls, along with pages torn from

Artelia Bendolph in the window of her house, 1937.

magazines and catalogs, not as art but as protection from drafts and the cold.

The families were tenant farmers, and rented their farms. Typically, tenant farmers payed the rent for the land and house by giving the owner a portion of the harvest. They didn't have enough money to buy seed and household supplies in the town of Camden across the Alabama River. The storekeepers gave them credit until harvest time—but they charged the farmers interest. So the farmers owed money to merchants for their purchases. When the harvest was good, the people of Gee's Bend got by. But when the price of cotton fell and dropped to a nickel a pound in the late 1920s, the Benders couldn't pay their debts. In 1932, one of the white merchants died without leaving records of who owed what. In the fall, his widow sent henchmen to Gee's Bend to collect from the entire community. The men swept in and took everything of value: cows, pigs, mules, farm equipment, tools, even stored sweet potatoes and

Lucy Mooney and granddaughters Lucy P. Pettway and Bertha Pettway on a bed in Lucy's house, 1937.

Houston Kennedy plowing on his farm, 1937.

peanuts. Mary Lee Bendolph, born three years later, recalled her mother telling how her father sat on the floor and wept. "Don't cry," Mary Lee's mother told him. "Everything be all right."

But it wasn't. "They were left starving to death," said Bill Jones, head of a Red Cross team. The Red Cross sent bags of flour and cornmeal by boat to the isolated community. The donations barely sustained the families. That winter, people survived by eating wild plums and berries, hunting deer, and fishing.

"They were very poor," said Tinne Dell Pettway, remembering her relatives. "Practically everybody down here was poor, and they shared with their neighbors."

"We went through some rough times," recalled Annie Mae Young. "You needed fire to keep warm. You can't quilt cold."

Then, in 1935, during the years of the Great Depression, President Franklin D. Roosevelt established a program to aid struggling farm families: the New

Deal. A journalist named Beverly Smith wrote about the poverty in Gee's Bend and the houses of "mud and stakes." She sent her article to Roy Stryker, head of a department in the federal government's Information Division. Stryker organized a team of photographers to take pictures of Gee's Bend and report on conditions there. Some of the photos showed women quilting in their cabins and sitting on beds covered with quilts, and making chair covers out of old flour sacks.

As a result of the report, in 1937, the government bought the old Pettway plantation. They divided the land into small farms and helped the Gee's Bend families buy the farms and build so-called Roosevelt houses, named for the president who had introduced the plan. With a government loan through the New Deal, Mary Lee Bendolph's grandfather bought a mule. A Cooperative was formed with government funds to establish a general store, a cotton gin, and a medical center. Families paid annual dues to

Lucy Mooney sewing a quilt in her living room with granddaughters Lucy P. Pettway and Bertha Pettway, 1937.

the Cooperative, and they shared its resources. A community school was also built. Up until then, the only school classes had been held in the Pleasant Grove Baptist Church for two or three months in the winter, because children were needed for harvesting and planting at other times. At the new school, first graders ranged in age from six to twenty-two. The school was managed by Wilcox County, where Gee's Bend was located. The county hired more teachers, and by 1944, the school had seven teachers and ten grades.

Jessie T. Pettway was nine when the school opened in 1938. From then on, she called herself Jessie after her favorite teacher. Jessie said, "We'd do our chores every morning before school, clean up the room and milk the cow, and after we'd get back, we'd do our homework. Then Little Sis—that's what we called my aunt Seebell [who was raising Jessie

Pleasant Grove Baptist Church, which doubled as the schoolhouse, 1937.

ABOVE Jessie T. Pettway, 2000.
RIGHT "Housetop," circa 1975, Qunnie Pettway.

and her siblings]—she'd give us lessons on how to cut out pieces and piece up quilts and help her quilt her own quilts, and that's how I learned."

Although conditions improved in Gee's Bend, the Roosevelt houses lacked indoor plumbing, running water, and electricity. The women still worked ten-hour days in the field and then returned home to fix supper and quilt. Even under these hard circumstances, each quilter came up with incredible versions of standard patterns.

"Ought not two quilts ever be the same," explained Mensie Lee Pettway.

Qunnie Pettway's "Housetop," for instance, is composed of only two colors: vivid red and pale

"Housetop," twenty-block variation, circa 1960, Nettie Jane Kennedy.

"Housetop," nine-block "Half-Log Cabin" variation, circa 1975, Jessie T. Pettway.

peach. The rectangular strips form a huge, powerful target. Nettie Jane Kennedy's "Housetop," however, appears to be rows of framed paintings. Each square within a square holds a different pattern—pale blue flowers, red blossoms—framed by more patterns.

Jessie T. Pettway worked to outdo herself with every "Housetop" quilt. One has such dazzling

"Texas Star," 1973, Ella Mae Irby.

"Blazing Star" with "Pinwheel" corner blocks, 1968, Lucy T. Pettway.

strips of colors and patterns—stars, plaids, paisleys, flowers—that it is hard to see the embedded nine squares. But her "Housetop" done in softer shades and framed in light gold corduroy more clearly shows the traditional number of blocks.

And then there are the star patterns. "Texas Star" by Ella Mae Irby explodes in pinks and browns and floral prints. Lucy T. Pettway's "Blazing Star" pulsates

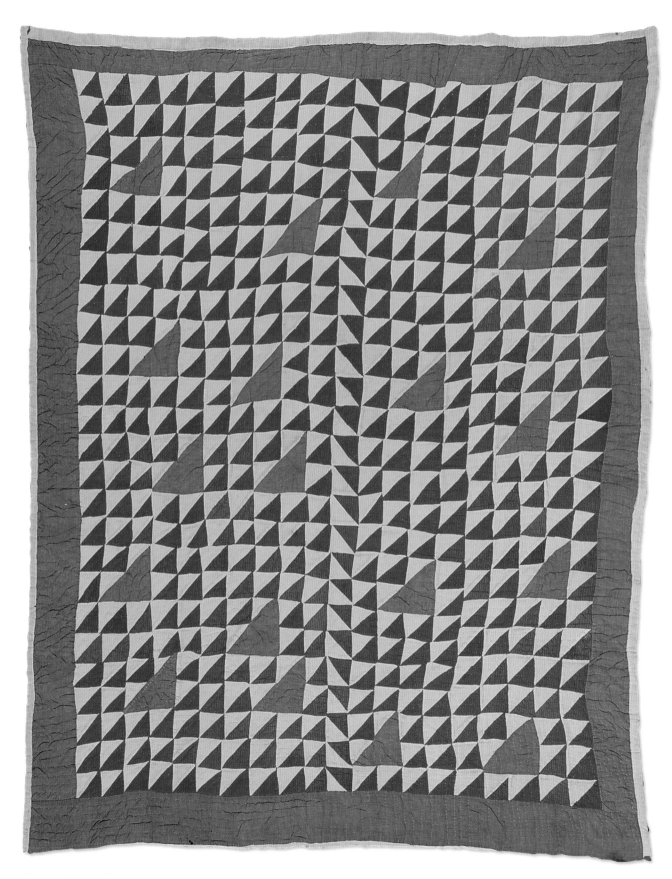

"Thousand Pyramids" variation, circa 1930, Annie Bendolph.

ABOVE Annie Bendolph, carrying water in front of her house on the Pettway plantation land, 1937.

RIGHT Blocks and stripes work-clothes quilt, 1942, Missouri Pettway.

from its red star in the center to its purple and green pinwheel corners.

As for designs based on triangles, each quilt is a surprise. Annie Bendolph's "Thousand Pyramids," featuring sacking material and chambray from worn shirts, flickers like a piece of op art.

Many "britches quilts" hold memories. "Old clothes carry something with them," said Mary Lee Bendolph. "You can feel the presence of the person who used to wear them. It has a spirit in them."

When Missouri Pettway's husband died in 1942 after a long illness, she made a quilt from his field trousers. She said, "I going to take his work clothes, shape them into a quilt to remember him, and cover

"Housetop," nine-block "Half-Log Cabin" variation, circa 1955, Sue Willie Seltzer.

up under it for love." Her daughter Arlonzia, then a teenager, assisted her and later described her mother's process: "She take his old pants legs and shirttails, take all the clothes he had, just enough to make that quilt, and I helped her tore them up." After Missouri died years later, Arlonzia saved the quilt in memory of both her parents.

During the next decades, from the 1940s on, the women kept quilting. They made tops by "piecing" the fabric together at home, and prepared backing layers. A quilt backing or bottom could be a sheet of fabric in a coordinated color. Or it may be an entirely different design, like Essie Bendolph Pettway's "One Patch" quilt, which has blue and white bars on one side and a riot of colors on the other. Once the two sewn pieces were done, it was time to stitch them together around batting to make the quilt. Bettie Bendolph Seltzer explained, "The ladies . . . go to each other house to help quilt."

"Quilt one or two for one person, go to the next house, do the same thing," recalled Sue Willie Seltzer. "From house to house, quilting quilts."

"They had to beat the cotton [with a stick] to pad it out to put in the quilt," Bettie said. "Their husband or friend or neighbor bring cotton from the gin for the ladies to quilt with."

Mary Lee Bendolph quilting her quilt top in her home, 2005.

"You beat the cotton out on the floor, first thing, to get the dust out," explained Mary Lee Bendolph. "Then sweep the floor—collect the cotton—spread the lining out and put the cotton back on the lining, beat it out, put the top on there, get your thread and needles and hook it in the quilting frame."

Grouped around the frame, the women basted the layers with the batting in between, and then they stitched.

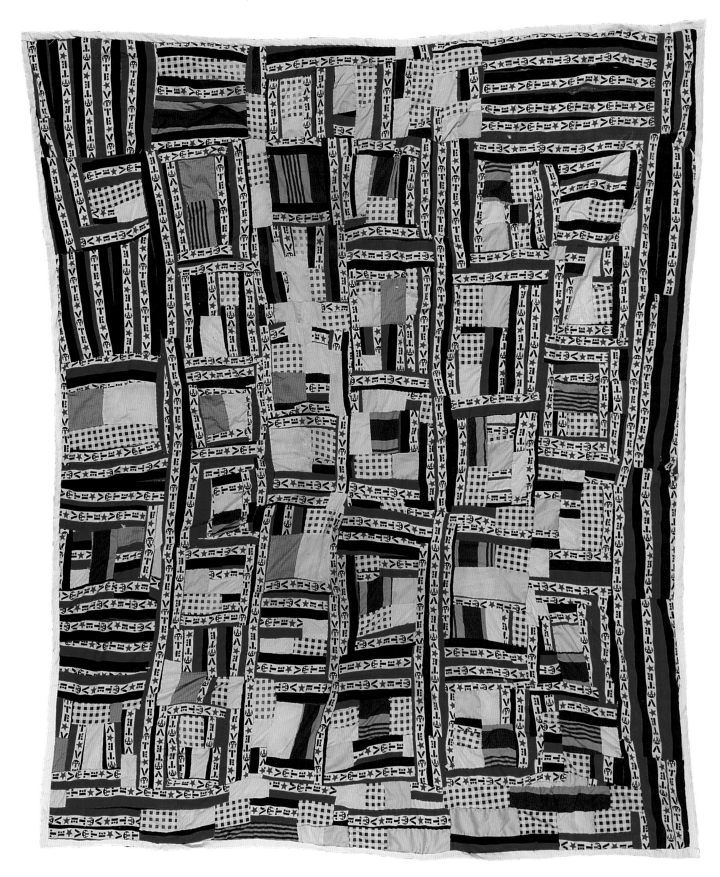

Irene Williams made several quilts that contain fabric printed with the word "vote." "Housetop" variation, circa 1975.

"We'd get together and make the quilts just like we're praying together," recalled Mary Lee Bendolph. Stitching and pulling, the women sang hymns and spirituals, and the quilts echoed their rhythms.

Every Sunday, the women attended Pleasant Grove Baptist Church with their families. Weekly sermons included political discussions based on bible lessons. People in Gee's Bend were struggling for civil rights along with African Americans throughout the Deep South. In Alabama, black people had to take an impossibly difficult "literacy test" and pay a poll tax in order to register to vote. Black people who had dared to try to register to vote had lost their jobs as farmers. White farm owners wanted to maintain the rules of segregation. Blacks knew that the key to challenging unjust laws was the vote.

Irene Williams made quilts that carried an uplifting message. Her red, white, and blue "Housetop" quilt contains bands of fabric printed with the word VOTE. "I remember when Martin Luther King came down here," she said. It was on a rainy night in February 1965. Dr. King was leading a voting rights campaign in Alabama. He had heard about Gee's Bend and stopped to preach at the Pleasant Grove Baptist Church.

When he stepped out of his car, Mary Lee Bendolph was one of the first to greet him. "I opened the door to the church," she said. "I was so glad to see that man. . . . And when he stood up and talked, I listened. . . . I didn't miss nothing."

Inspired by the huge turnout, Dr. King said, "To come here to Gee's Bend and to see you out in large numbers gives me new courage and new determination.

"I come over here to Gee's Bend to tell you: You are somebody."

Amelia Bennett couldn't get to the church that night, but she heard stories about the sermon. "It made me feel very good, the path he cut for us," she recalled. "It was . . . like you walk into a room and ain't no light on, and you turn on a light in the darkness—that's what Dr. King meant to us. He turned on the light for us."

Dr. King urged the congregation to join him in Camden to march to the courthouse for voting rights. Camden, a nearly all-white town, was the seat of Wilcox County and the place where people registered to vote and cast their ballots. However, no African American had ever voted in Wilcox County. "I had to beg my husband to let me go," said Mary Lee Bendolph. "But I went. We rode on Monroe Pettway's truck."

Old cable ferry between Camden and Gee's Bend, Alabama, 1939.

Arlonzia Pettway said, "Lots of people from Gee's Bend were going over to register to vote." Many took the ferry—merely a creaky raft poled by Uncle Linzie, an old-timer. It was the quickest way to get to Camden, and most Benders didn't have cars.

One week later, the ferry was shut down. "Some of the white people said it had nothing to do with the marching," recalled Arlonzia. "But it sure did. After that, we kept right on marching. Only difference was we had to load up in trucks and drive all the way around."

Two weeks after the rally, a few Gee's Bend women joined Dr. King's voting rights crusade in Selma. Mary Lee Bendolph said, "I was in the group with Martin Luther King when he went up to drink the 'white' water." In those days of Jim Crow segregation, there were signs on restaurants, buses, and water fountains that said "White Only" or "Colored Only." "He [Dr. King] wanted us to know the water wasn't no different and to let the white people know that we could all drink the same water," said Mary Lee. "I never saw a black person do a thing like that. I was so glad. So I went up to drink me some of it." Her oldest sister, Lillie Mae, worried that she'd get hurt and pulled her away. But Mary Lee finally tasted the "white water" and said, "It wasn't no different. I wondered what all the fussing was about."

Lucy Mingo and Estelle Witherspoon marched with Dr. King from Selma to Montgomery. "No white man gonna tell me not to march," declared Lucy. "Only make me march harder."

Because of the protest demonstrations and attempts to register to vote, many black families in Possum Bend, on the Camden side of the river, were forced out of their houses by their white landlords. Banks owned by whites foreclosed on loans to black people and took back their houses. Most Benders in their part of Wilcox County owned their Roosevelt houses and hung on to them.

In December 1965, a civil-rights worker named Father Francis Xavier Walter came to hear the stories of people in Possum Bend and help them. Noticing some patchwork quilts hanging on a clothesline, he

Lucy Mingo, 2000.

grew interested and started asking questions. Father Walter was directed to Gee's Bend.

Once a year, the women in Gee's Bend hung their quilts on fences and clotheslines to "air out." They enjoyed going from house to house to view one another's work. "It was just like going to a museum," recalled Mary Lee Bendolph.

Quilts hanging on the line, 2006.

Her daughter Essie said, "Boy, you could see [the quilts] a good ways off the highway. And they was beautiful and they had such a radiant color to them . . . a color that would just take your attention away . . . just have you amazed."

Father Walter *was* amazed. Astonished. He began buying quilts to send to New York City, where they would be auctioned. The proceeds would go to the Gee's Bend community. But as he talked to the women, he came up with the idea of organizing a sewing cooperative to help them earn money. So in 1966, sixty quilt makers met with him in Camden and founded the Freedom Quilting Bee. In the beginning, they quilted at Estelle Witherspoon's house.

Leola Pettway (left) and Qunnie Pettway (right) working at the Freedom Quilting Bee. Leola is making a "Bear Paw" while Qunnie makes a "Rik-Rak," 1972.

"The Bee was the first business black people in Wilcox County owned," said Nettie Young, one of the original members. "It was the first time I knew I was special, the first job I had—excusing cotton picking."

Meanwhile, the quilts that Father Walker had bought were auctioned in New York. Celebrities from the art world bought them. Painter Lee Krasner, wife of Jackson Pollock, visited Gee's Bend in 1967 to watch the women quilting, and she ordered three quilts. "It was quite a sight to behold," she wrote.

At first, the Bee stitched and sold unique quilts along with potholders, aprons, and sunbonnets. Two years later, a crafts marketer arranged a contract with

Willie "Ma Willie" Abrams, unidentified photographer, 1970s.

Willie "Ma Willie" Abrams, shared her beautiful pattern blocks and designs.

"Used to worry me to death trying to make every quilt just like this, just like that, but I did," recalled Arlonzia Pettway. But the buyers at Bloomingdale's complained about uneven workmanship. "A lot of those quilts came back," said Arlonzia. "They had to be did over. That drive you crazy."

Nettie Young said, "In the Quilting Bee time, I started using patterns, but I shouldn't have did it. It broke the ideas I had in my head. I should have stayed with my own ideas."

Annie Mae Young decided not to join the Bee. "They didn't want the kind of sewing and piecing I do," she said, "and I didn't like what they was doing. They had to do things too particular, too careful, too many little blocks. So I never did have nothing to do with them."

But business grew, and the Bee kept busy. In March 1969, they constructed a sewing center halfway between Gee's Bend and the town of Alberta. At the groundbreaking, the center was dedicated to the memory of Dr. Martin Luther King, Jr., who had been assassinated on April 4, 1968. Afterward, a service was held at Pleasant Grove Baptist Church, where he had preached just three years before.

Bloomingdale's department store in New York. There were new standards. And new fabrics. All the quilts had to be the same. Estelle Witherspoon's mother,

The contract with Bloomingdale's fizzled out as the department store lost interest. Starting in 1972 and for the next twenty years, the Bee produced corduroy pillow covers for Sears, Roebuck & Company. The women also made baby quilts for Saks Fifth Avenue and Bonwit Teller, leading department stores in New York City. But their output for stores didn't affect their startling originality. They continued making their own unique quilts in the late 1960s and afterward, using leftover swatches of Sears corduroy. The material inspired fresh ideas.

In 1975, Flora Moore made a "Log Cabin" variation completely in corduroy. "It was cheap and it was heavy," she said about the fabric. "You didn't need to put much batting in it to keep warm." That same year, "Ma Willie" Abrams stitched a spectacular "Roman Stripes" quilt. It features blocks of corduroy strips in deep red, orange, olive green, blue, and chocolate brown.

Linda Pettway did a corduroy "Housetop" quilt in orangey red and soft shades of cream, ivory, and tan. "I loved to make my own patterns," she said. "I just get the cloth, cut the pieces, lay it out on the bed. . . . I start in the middle . . . keep going 'round the sides. I be knowing where I'm going."

The women kept quilting, but other than a few

Corduroy pillow covers as they appeared on page 1494 of the Fall and Winter Sears catalog, 1974.

retailers, outsiders had stopped paying attention to Gee's Bend and the quilt makers.

Then, during the late 1970s and early '80s, collec-

"Roman Stripes" variation, circa 1975, Willie "Ma Willie" Abrams.

tor Bill Arnett was researching African American art in the South. He loved rock 'n' roll, gospel, blues, and jazz—music that had originated in the South. Bill believed there must be visual art that was waiting to be discovered. He and his son, Matt, drove from town to town exploring and gathering artwork by self-taught African American artists. Most of them were men.

One day in 1998, Bill saw a photo in a book on African American quilters by Roland Freeman that captivated him. The picture showed Annie Mae Young with a quilt she had made draped over a woodpile in her yard. "Wow!" said Bill. "Let's go find that woman."

Armed with the book, he and Matt set out. When they finally arrived at Annie Mae's house on the outskirts of Gee's Bend, she was surprised. She had never seen the book with a picture of her and her quilt, so Bill gave her his copy. "What happened to

Annie Mae Young with quilts and her great-granddaughter Shaquetta, Rehoboth, 1993.

that quilt?" he asked. She thought she had burned it to make room for others. But she allowed the Arnetts to look through her house. At last she called, "I think I found it!" and offered to give it to them. Bill insisted on paying for it.

"Some other people down here make quilts," said Annie Mae, and she sent them to six other houses. From then on, the Arnetts kept going back to Gee's Bend and were introduced to 150 quilt makers. They spent hundreds of dollars on old quilts. The women thought they were crazy. To them, the quilts were "something to cover up with." They didn't think of themselves as artists, but Bill recognized their work as some of the best art in the country. He founded the Tinwood Alliance, a nonprofit organization, to collect and preserve the quilts. Matt took photographs. Bill showed the pictures to people in the art world and talked passionately about the women's quilts. "It's important," he said. "Study it. Show it."

Many museums and galleries weren't interested. Then, in 2002, Bill and Matt were working with the Museum of Fine Arts, Houston, on another project. They found out that an exhibit that had been scheduled for that year was canceled. To fill the slot, the museum agreed to show seventy of the Gee's Bend quilts.

The exhibit opened on September 8, 2002. In the book accompanying the show, the director of the museum praised the quilts as "works of art." He wrote, "These women learn from one another but strive to be themselves."

The public flocked to the show and loved it. From Houston, the exhibit traveled to New York City's Whitney Museum. Crowds thronged the museum, breaking attendance records. Art critics wrote rave reviews. Michael Kimmelman of the *New York Times* described the quilts as "eye-poppingly gorgeous." He said they were "some of the most miraculous works of modern art America has produced" and told readers if they didn't believe him, go and see the show for themselves. The exhibit went on to museums in Boston, Atlanta, and San Francisco.

Thousands of copies of the illustrated book were printed and quickly sold out. The book was reprinted many times. Proceeds from the book sales were shared between the quilt makers and Tinwood Alliance. With income generated by the sale of the book, the women were able to make improvements to their homes. Loretta Pettway got indoor plumbing and added on to her house. Some of the quilters like Annie Mae Young and Arlonzia Pettway had given up quilting because of arthritis and bad eyesight due to old age, but seeing their work celebrated inspired

Medallion, circa 1960, Loretta Pettway, reattributed to unknown.

them to start again. Nettie Young began teaching her twenty-nine-year-old granddaughter how to quilt.

Nettie, age ninety, said, "Martin Luther King got us out of the cotton patch; the Arnetts got us out from under the bedsprings and onto the museum walls."

Mensie Lee Pettway said, "A lot of people make quilts for your bed, for to keep you warm. But a quilt is more. It represents safekeeping, it represents beauty, and you could say it represents family history."

"H" variation, quilt maker's name: "Milky Way," 1971, Nettie Young.

Epilogue

After the huge success of the traveling museum exhibit, the Gee's Bend Quilters Collective was formed in 2003 with the assistance of Tinwood Alliance. The Collective helped the women sell some of their quilts to museums and individuals. Half of every sale went to the quilter and the other half went to the Collective, which distributed the payment among the members, some of whom could no longer sew.

In 2006, a set of US postal stamps featuring eight quilts of Gee's Bend was issued as part of the American Treasures series and the quilts were featured in calendars and on greeting cards.

The attention given to the Gee's Bend quilts sparked jealousy and controversy. Some people in the community and children of the older quilters felt that they weren't fairly compensated for their work. Attorneys for Annie Mae Young and Loretta Pettway filed a suit against the Arnetts in 2007. However, forty quilt makers refused to join the lawsuit. Most of the Gee's Bend women were extremely satisfied and grateful to the Arnetts. In 2008, the case was dismissed.

Bill went on to establish the Souls Grown Deep Foundation, dedicated to researching, preserving, and exhibiting art by African Americans. Recently, the Foundation gave a gift of fifty-seven works to the Metropolitan Museum of Art in New York. The gift includes twenty quilts from Gee's Bend.

Making a Quilt Square

Here's a simple way to make your own quilt square that will measure 12" x 12" (30.5 cm x 30.5 cm). A bed quilt will need many squares, but a baby quilt needs only nine squares.

To make a baby quilt, you'll need a total of nine squares to make a quilt that measures 36" (91 cm). After you have completed the nine individual squares you will sew them together, as described in steps 3 and 4.

More directions on how to turn squares into a quilt can be found in quilting books and on the Internet.

SUPPLIES:

ONE LARGE PIECE OF FABRIC, AT LEAST 12½" X 12½"

   (31.75 CM X 31.75 CM)

ONE RULER

ONE PENCIL

ONE PAIR OF SCISSORS

STRAIGHT PINS

ONE NEEDLE

THREAD

DIRECTIONS:

2.

1. First, choose your fabric. You will want to have a nice, large piece to work from—you can use old clothes, a ragged dish towel, a worn-out apron, or scraps from another project. Take your ruler, and mark six 12½" (31.75 cm) long lines on your fabric with your pencil, 2½" (6.3 cm) apart.

2. Cut along the long lines with your scissors to create six strips measuring 12½" x 2½" (31.75 cm x 6.3 cm). The women of Gee's Bend often tore the strips, but it's easier to cut with scissors.

3. Look at your fabric. The side with the design is called the "right side" and the back is called the "wrong side." Use your straight pins to pin two of the strips together with their "right sides" touching (the wrong side should be facing up). Thread your needle, and use it to sew the pieces together ¼" (6 mm) away from the long edge to the right with a small running stitch. Try to keep the stitches in a straight line as you sew. This stitched section is called a "seam." Remove the pins.

3.

1 2 1 2 1 2 1 2 1 2 1 2 1 2 1

1 - needle back to front

2 - needle front to back

4.

4. Open the strips so that the "right sides" are facing up. Pin a third strip to the strip on the right of the two that you've already stitched, with "right sides" touching again. Sew it on in the same way. Repeat this for each strip.

5. After you've stitched all six strips together, you have a square that measures 12½" x 12½" (31.75 cm x 31.75 cm).

6. To make it smooth, turn it over and press the seams either open or to the side with an iron so that they lie flat.

5.

"Log Cabin," "Housetop" bars and blocks, circa 1955, Lucy T. Pettway.

Notes

Page 6: "When I was . . . made your quilts." *The Quilts of Gee's Bend* (video).

Page 7: "I always loved . . . the way I want it." Beardsley et al, *Gee's Bend: The Women and Their Quilts*, 184.

Page 7: "Didn't nobody teach . . . want them to look." Beardsley et al, *The Quilts of Gee's Bend*, 116.

Page 7: "work like slaves for the white people." *The Quilts of Gee's Bend* (video).

Page 8: "We had no radio . . . more blessed then." Brown, "From the Bottomlands, Soulful Stitches."

Page 8: "I was looking . . . for myself." Beardsley et al, *Gee's Bend: The Women and Their Quilts*, 33.

Page 8: "When we got nine . . . we quilted so much." *The Quilts of Gee's Bend* (video).

Page 12: "I just made . . . and stuff." Beardsley et al, *The Quilts of Gee's Bend*, 73.

Page 14: "You find the colors . . . a puzzle." Beardsley et al, *The Quilts of Gee's Bend*, 100.

Page 14: "You could see . . . through the wall." Beardsley et al, *The Quilts of Gee's Bend*, 26.

Page 16: "Don't cry . . . all right." Beardsley et al, *The Quilts of Gee's Bend*, 24.

Page 16: "They were left . . . to death." Beardsley et al, *The Quilts of Gee's Bend*, 24.

Page 16: "They were very . . . shared with their neighbors." *Gee's Bend: The Women and Their Quilts*, 238.

Page 16: "We went through . . . quilt cold." Brown, "From the Bottomlands, Soul Stitches."

Page 17: "mud and stakes." Beardsley et al, *Gee's Bend: The Women and Their Quilts*, 27.

Page 18: "We'd do our . . . how I learned." Beardsley et al, *The Quilts of Gee's Bend*, 88.

Page 19: "Ought not . . . be the same." Beardsley et al, *The Quilts of Gee's Bend*, 18.

Page 25: "Old clothes . . . spirit in them." Arnett et al, *Gee's Bend: The Architecture of the Quilt*, 74.

Page 25: "I was going to . . . her tore them up." Beardsley et al, *The Quilts of Gee's Bend*, 67.

Page 27: "the ladies . . . to help quilt." Beardsley et al, *Gee's Bend: The Women and Their Quilts*, 222.

Page 27: "Quilt one or . . . quilting quilts." Beardsley et al, *The Quilts of Gee's Bend*, 124.

Page 27: "They had to beat . . . to quilt with." Beardsley et al, *Gee's Bend: The Women and their Quilts*, 222.

Page 27: "You beat . . . quilting frame." Beardsley et al, *Gee's Bend: The Women and Their Quilts*, 254, and *The Quilts of Gee's Bend*, 128.

Page 29: "We'd get together . . . praying together." Brown, "From the Bottomlands, Soul Stitches."

Page 29: "I remember . . . came down here." Beardsley et al, *The Quilts of Gee's Bend*, 126.

Page 29: "I opened . . . didn't miss nothing." Beardsley et al, *The Quilts of Gee's Bend*, 130.

Page 29: "To come here . . . new determination." Beardsley et al, *The Quilts of Gee's Bend*, 31.

Page 29: "I come here . . . are somebody." Moehringer, "Crossing Over."

Page 29: "It made me . . . light for us." Beardsley et al, *The Quilts of Gee's Bend*, 82.

Page 29: "I had to beg . . . Pettway's truck." Beardsley et al, *The Quilts of Gee's Bend*, 130.

Page 30: "Lots of people . . . to vote." Beardsley et al, *The Quilts of Gee's Bend*, 33.

Page 30: "Some of the . . . the way around." Beardsley et al, *The Quilts of Gee's Bend*, 31.

Page 30: "I was in the . . . fussing was about." Beardsley et al, *The Quilts of Gee's Bend*, 130.

Page 31: "No white man . . . march harder." Beardsley et al, *The Quilts of Gee's Bend*, 31.

Page 31: "It was just . . . a museum." Cubbs et al, *Mary Lee Bendolph, Gee's Bend Quilts and Beyond*, 28.

Page 32: "Boy, you could see . . . have you amazed." Cubbs et al, *Mary Lee Bendolph, Gee's Bend Quilts and Beyond*, 29.

Page 33: "The Bee was . . . cotton picking." Brown, "From the Bottomlands, Soul Stitches."

Page 33: "It was . . . to behold." Beardsley et al, *The Quilts of Gee's Bend*, 54.

Page 34: "Used to worry . . . drive you crazy." Beardsley et al, *The Quilts of Gee's Bend*, 32.

Page 34: "In the Quilting . . . my own ideas." Beardsley et al, *Gee's Bend: The Women and Their Quilts*, 366.

Page 34: "They didn't want . . . do with them." Beardsley et al, *The Quilts of Gee's Bend*, 100.

Page 35: "It was cheap . . . keep warm." Beardsley et al, *Gee's Bend: The Women and Their Quilts*, 408.

Page 35: "I loved to . . . where I'm going." Beardsley et al, *The Quilts of Gee's Bend*, 160.

Page 37: "Wow! . . . that woman." Matt Arnett, interview with author.

Page 37: "What happened . . . found it!" Matt Arnett, interview with author.

Page 38: "Some other people . . . make quilts." Matt Arnett, interview with author.

Page 38: "something to cover up with." Herman, "The Quilts of Gee's Bend."

Page 38: "It's important . . . Show it." Bill Arnett, interview with author.

Page 38: "works of art . . . to be themselves." Beardsley et al, *Gee's Bend: The Women and Their Quilts*, 9.

Page 38: "eye-poppingly . . . has produced." Kimmelman, "Jazzy Geometry, Cool Quilters."

Page 39: "Martin Luther King . . . onto the museum walls." Dewan, "Handmade Alabama Quilts Find Fame and Controversy."

Page 39: "A lot of people . . . represents family history." Beardsley et al, *The Quilts of Gee's Bend*, 18.

Bibliography

Books

Note: An asterisk denotes books suitable for younger readers.

Arnett, William, Louisiana P. Bendolph, Mary Lee Bendolph, Loretta P. Bennett, Dilys Blum, Joanne Cubbs, Maggi McCormick Gordon, Bernard L. Herman, Amei Wallach, Lauren Whitley. *Gee's Bend: The Architecture of the Quilt.* Atlanta, Georgia: Tinwood Books, 2006.

Beardsley, William Arnett, Paul Arnett, Jane Livingston. *Gee's Bend: The Women and Their Quilts.* Atlanta, Georgia: Tinwood Books, 2002.

Beardsley, John, William Arnett, Paul Arnett, Jane Livingston. *The Quilts of Gee's Bend.* Atlanta, Georgia: Tinwood Books, 2002.

Cubbs, Joanne, Matt Arnett, and Dana Friis-Hansen. *Mary Lee Bendolph, Gee's Bend Quilts and Beyond.* Atlanta: Tinwood Books/Austin Museum of Art, 2006.

*Marsh, Carole. *Gee's Bend Quilts.* Carole Marsh Books, Gallopade International, 2006.

*McKissack, Patricia C. *Stitchin' and Pullin': A Gee's Bend Quilt.* New York: Random House Children's Books, 2008.

Articles

Brown, Patricia Leigh. "From the Bottomlands, Soulful Stitches." *New York Times,* November 21, 2002.

Dewan, Shaila. "Handmade Alabama Quilts Find Fame and Controversy." *New York Times*, July 29, 2007.

Dunner, Shermika and Erin Z. Bass, "The Future of Gee's Bend." *Deep South Magazine*, April 17, 2012.

Herman, Bernard L. "The Quilts of Gee's Bend: How Great Art Gets Lost." *Journal of Modern Craft*, Souls Grown Deep Foundation, March 2009.

Kimmelman, Michael. "Jazzy Geometry, Cool Quilters." *New York Times*, November 29, 2002.

Moehringer, J. R. "Crossing Over." *Los Angeles Times*, August 22, 1999.

Videos

The Quilts of Gee's Bend. Souls Grown Deep Foundation. Tinwood Media, 2006.

Internet Sources

"The Ferry Is Coming." Martin Luther King, Jr. quoted in a film clip. *60 Minutes II*, July 4, 2000.

Haberman, Clyde. "The Ferry: a Civil Rights Story." Retro Report, *New York Times* online, March 9, 2015.

Stephanos, Mary. "The Quilts of Gee's Bend Speak Eloquently of Lives Lived." USPS Stamps Blog, February 4, 2012. http://uspsstamps. com/blog/2012/2/4.

Author Interviews

Bill Arnett, June 4, 2015.

Matt Arnett, June 4, 2015.

Acknowledgments

I am deeply grateful to the quilters of Gee's Bend for allowing us to show some of their magnificent work and to tell their stories. My sincerest thanks to William and Matt Arnett of the Souls Grown Deep Foundation for making this book possible. And a big thank you to Laura Bickford for her help with images. I also express gratitude to Julian Cox, founding curator of photography for the Fine Arts Museums of San Francisco and chief curator at the de Young Museum, for providing contact information.

At Abrams I want to thank my editor Howard Reeves for his enthusiastic support; Orlando Dos Reis, assistant editor; Melissa J. Barrett, our talented designer; Jason Wells in Marketing; and Jen Graham, a skillful managing editor.

I will always be indebted to my friend, mentor, and agent George Nicholson (1937–2015), who inspired me with his passionate interest in the Gee's Bend quilts and African American folk art. I thank my writer friends at Lunch Bunch and Third Act for their ongoing encouragement. And I especially appreciate Ann Whitford Paul's lesson in how to make a quilt square.

Susan Goldman Rubin
Malibu, California

Image Credits

Index

Note: Page numbers in *italics* refer to illustrations.